INTUITION

DOMINIC ANTON

Cover design by
Marissa Anton

Illustrations & Photography by
Dominic Anton
Marissa Anton
Mario Manzanares

ISBN-13: 978- 1087856704
ISBN-10: 1725692813

For those lost in the
waves of this world

Oh the heart
is so heavy
weighing on my
watered world

I've always sought comfort in nature. Hidden under green canopies of palm leaves, far away from crowds. I have closed my eyes, listened to the birds up above. The wind brushing through the leaves, in otherwise total silence. I've sought peace in the stillness, silencing my mind. Preparing myself. Although these days are numbered as each tree gets cut down, shrinking my piece of paradise, I'm conditioning, repairing myself again from the dirt, not for the end, but planting each seed, for a new beginning.

- The Forest

Pushed and pulled through tides, sinking my head in crystal waters near the pier, wondering how to pause time. Each day and night, from rooftops to the oceans drive as we run through streets, with bloodshot eyes and wild. Rolling blue dreams and smoking through our problems, drinking the day and pouring the night. Happiness always seemed out of reach, though we caught it for a moment, slipping out of sanity under the sunsets glow. Ready and relentless,

Everything Was Beautiful

I can lose myself in all our laughs,
That ring so loud, though never lasts.
Broken records, repeating ourselves,
Like witches casting broken spells.
Life is a glorious goal in itself,
Though sometimes I can never tell.
Losing friends, new cities, new lives,
Until I give my final sigh.

- Impermanence

C'est
L'amour-o
La plage!

Falling in and out love,
From the shadows of the bars,
To the rooftops of downtown.
The nights left on repeat with
Polluted, dancing bodies
In the midnights moon.
Chasers race to knock
Us down on dance floors.
Lighting up on the oceans
Drive, in the stretches of
The onyx sea, together. But
Miami is sinking,
Miami is burning,
All the days we cannot hold
Anymore. fading forever.

- Miami is Burning

I don't want to speak.
Hallucinating in the heat.
I don't want to hear.
Levitating in the clouds.
Sweating out each thought.
Bending back into the waters.
Isolated, watching all the
Vibrant, dripping colors.
Teal, lavender, ice mint too.
And all that was felt,
'til my mind froze blue.
But I don't want to hear.
Now I don't want to speak.
Underneath my tongue,

Hallucinating

I need to do things to feel more alive,
Take drugs to widen my eyes,
Paint days to move from
The greys,
The ways,
We're living today,
Is killing us slowly,
In these altered states.

I live my life as if I'm on display,
The judgment is never away,
The clouds rolling rain
To the sea,
I think,
That most everything,
Is just an illusion,
To keep us happy.

We're driving,
We're headed,
Down the wrong dream.

-    Wasted

The hot whips of reality,
Crack in summer heat, over lies,
And all else that I always
Thought would be.

Although I always knew,
That I would see the day,
Blood runs down my back,
Now that everything
Washed away.

-    Liminality

My eyes are red,
Dripping with salted secrets.
In the deepest way, I had a taste,
But slipped on my confusion.
With communication breaking over each
Turn, each breath, two souls split
After obligated discourse.
I thought it was what
I wanted, but with just a touch,
We turned to ash.
Arrived and went,
As strangers.

-    Loss & Longing

Cut the ropes to finally breathe,
No more wasting energy.
Nothing cruel, but
I still need, some space,
You know you're
Dead to me.

Roses only bloom to die
and nothing ever lasts in life.
Tell me one more lie,
I'll say goodbye,
You're

Dead To Me

Wrung out and standing over the edge of freedom.
A sighing death, into the void. The ocean had flooded
All I know, carrying away my haven, friends, routine.
Responsibility left with empty hands and blank canvases.
Silence is pressing.
Future uncertain.
Nowhere to turn to.
Back at square one.
Each question, each problem, the conflict and confusion, all
Eating me alive, ripping my flesh with incisors.
There's nowhere to go, but I still

Run

Strength is required to remove and detach yourself from what you've grown up in. The same house. The same streets. The same days stuck repeating themselves in the same skin. I've become stiff. I've stopped growing. I've yet to pinpoint what marks growth effectively as my growth comes and goes in sharp spurts up and landslides down, but I know the first sign of growth is when everything around me starts to rot. I start to turn on myself, no longer breathing air which has been polluted for so many years. I then start ripping everything down, packing up. I don't know if moving to a newer place either marks self-growth or merely presents you with illusions of change, however at this point, I need clear air.

There's nothing like the energy of an airport. The flying hearts of thousands of strangers, thousands of worlds, meeting together to part again. Flying over state lines and sky lines across earth. The excitement that makes my blood rush through each terminal, passing loved ones kissing goodbye and hugging hello. The eyes of intent and wonder skim through each sign and out the windows, waiting to board to a foreign land or back home. I think I'll be at airports flying forever, because

I don't know where home is anymore.

Every day and every wave
Of new experiences wash over me,
Filling my body with waters of a new world.
Widening my eyes and sinking
Into the deepest parts of my body,
Altering its chemistry.
This foreign water carries
Away the expired past as it takes control
Of me, and I then realized how
Thirsty I had been for so long.

-     WATERLUST

Deep within sacred seclusion.
Tuned into these conscious calls.
No voices, nor familiar hands.
Calls ignored, unbothered and still.
Dissociate in empty space,
Feel air leaving my lungs.
My heartbeat light,
In peace, in

Isolation

London's calling
Why won't you wake up?
The sky is falling,
Why can't you wake up?
The world is twisting, bending,
You can never escape,
Far from palm tree cities,
Yet you still feel the same.
Unfasten your seatbelt
Free fall, fuck it, fly away.
Time is never making sense,
Never measured anyway.

-       Immeasurable Madness

Into another country with
Certain differences, but same
Bleeding hearts. With
Crowds marching
Near Westminster, shouting,
Protecting, blood to be spared.
In stabled rage they try
To raise each other up.
With awareness higher
Than mankind has
Ever reached after
100 years, hopefully
Not 100 more, to
Make another shift.
But only with each other
And our voices we can
Change as fast as
Our hearts can fly.

- Revolutions

Your words reflect a broken heart,
Misunderstood and sinking.
Look for your face in Camden, stoned.
Out of my head, not thinking.
My dark friends all play pretend,
Believing that I'm fine.
Your words reflect, a troubled heart,
Wicked struggle of the minds.
No one to call, no local phone.
I still spin your records,
When I wake up alone.

    -    Amy

Slaves to the material,
Pull the weight of desire
Across deserts of heat.
Without judgment,
Without reason,
Nor their eyes to see.
Delusions dare,
To sway the masses,
Restrict them into
Programmed thoughts,
Where everything is nothing
And everything is bought.

-     Material

Solitude is the friend
I've never asked for, though I need.
Year after year, silencing the external,
Familiarizing the depths of my disposition,
Growing myself from the inside out, alone.
I love solitude. I pull down each grey
Cloud in London's icy skies, hiding
From the world in his embrace as I close
The door, shutting everything out.

COLDER THAN STONE
WEIGHING ON BONES
THE PRESSURING PLUMMET
OF POSITIVITY LOST, SEVERED,
DISCONNECTED. ALWAYS ONLY
MYSELF. A DARK REVERIE.
WISHING. DECAYING.

A dystopian world.

A society where aggression is commended, where hate has more power over love,
With blood staining each day, state to state. The pure and loving, have their mouths
sewn shut, Arms cut off. Firing guns, roses ripping in retaliation. It is the world, we
wake up to today, A world, of dark clouds raining blood from never ending storms.

-    Human Nature?

It always astounds me, the thought, the millions of people
we encounter in our lives. Complete strangers, yet commonalities
keeping us connected. With every glance and expression sparking
a certain feeling of wonder between us. Intrigued, with potential just
at the tip of our tongues.

Maybe we will meet, maybe we will just pass for a moment. Though
our energies shared, a smile, with no word spoken can still be enough
to remind that there is love everywhere. Through any storm,
through any dark day.

-     Unbreakable Bonds

looking in corners,
looking in bars,
looking in clubs,
underneath the lights.
searching through cities,
catching a stare,
a potential perfection,
broke by the dance.
searching, and hoping,
wishing and waiting,
for the truest reflection,
for the mirrored heart.

–   Soul Separate

What if..

My goals run too fast for me to ever catch up and all that is in
my head will remain on a loop, untranslated into reality.
Everything I want, everything I see, is simply just teasing me,
Far out of reach, no matter how high I climb. Instead, falling in a

Folie De Grandeur

Laying near the square,
Connection dead.
Problems on pause.
Giving the days to the sun,
Silencing my thoughts.
Far from what was known, incognito,
With lemon dripping down my mouth.
Mermaids watching and
Fountains spray above.
Burned cherry cheeks,
Parisian heat, daydreaming.

-    Proche Place de La Concorde

Je rêve toujours de toi,

mais tu pourrais être n'importe qui,

tu pourrais être n'importe où,

tu pourrais être n'importe quoi.

peut-être, pour autant que je sache,

tu ne pourrais être rien,

mais un limité

sentiment d'espoir.

I always dream of you,

But you could be anyone,

You could be anywhere,

You can be anything.

Perhaps, as far as I know,

You could be nothing,

But a limited feeling

Of hope.

\-   Rêver De Toi

champagne poured, all else forgotten.
three hearts through la vie en rose.
the shifting days, been put on pause,
the problems, the worry, erased.
In a lavender trance and saving
every sweet, rose-tinted state.
the city glows, happiness holds
the pleasure to escape.

-    La Vie En Rose

So smooth smoking, cigarette from your lips.
Heart is on fire, full flaming and drips.
Another shot to numb the pain,
Angels sing as heaven falls.
Another death among the day.
Sorrows pinned against the wall.
When I'm walking through
The streets, you somehow
Find your way to me.
In every moment,
Rest in roses,
Ma cherie.

- Edith

A single drop of nothing, in the beginning.

Pearls strung over determined minds, to bring visions closer to birth into reality. Our destiny. We are born into nothing. We live to try. fail. try. fail. try and keep working. Our passion does not allow failure, it does not allow us to merely give up. It is not in our blood, a confusing concept. Step by step. From dirt to diamonds. From ash to precious stone. As legacies live on, I will keep climbing, step by step, up the staircase. Each mirror pane reflecting each effort, each moment until I reach the highest step and meet her embrace. Then my creations could glow independently, in recognition, in appreciation, in peace.

– pour coco

Failure of success can be shattering,
But revival of effort is unbreakable.

mademoiselle,
    merci pour tout.
vous êtes le reve qui
renait en moi. l'energie
que je porte avec chaque
victoire et échec. je
continue à grimper. je
continue de travailler.

Through the thread,
Wishes sewn,
Every piece fits
In the sketches that
Blueprints destiny.
Hours of work, of
Writing, of sketching,
Sew buttons of effort,
Down years, aligned.
In fullest form, wear
Passions in pride.
Every piece shining,
Portraying each life.

-     Haute Couture

Gargoyles overhead in the heat of August. In the cobbled streets, certain that I lost myself. Lost my head in the trees, all the memories at least, like paintings in golden frames. New energies, absorbed, worn, tried. Changing scenes and unfamiliar feelings that cannot be described.

The seconds race off in the stretches of weeks, that turn and twist like an altering dream. Ever changing. Evergreen.

-     Eternal Changes

Most times I think I know myself,
Sometimes I know nothing at all.
Most times I keep to all my plans,
'Till expectations hit a wall.
Every day I wake to ritual,
Drink my blood
And eat my flesh.
Communing with myself,
Unlocked the chambers in my chest.
Darkworking deep within to
Know the soul, beneath the skin.
Down in these black waters,
I condition in the night.

- Coeur Noir

The way of the roses, they grow and die. Bear thorns, adorned, perfume the sky. Wrapped around gold gates, Versailles, 'til fountains run red with blood. All these roses, red to rotten. An entire garden of love, forgotten. But that's the truth, we bloom, we grow, until our summers meet the snow.

-    The Way of The Roses

I'm not worried anymore,
No, I'm not wasting any time.
There's nothing certain anymore.
Nothing's wrong and nothing's right.
I'm not hurting anymore.
I've forgotten all that's been.
Not interested defining who I am,
In clouds, drifting.

- Flight 1830

Across the oceans
Changing states,
Feelings are lost
And peace cascades.
Above the rocks
The salted air,
I see it glowing,
Standing there.
To give direction,
Give its light,
To clear the coldest,
Blackest night.
I'll swim up to,
With pure intentions,
The house, it lights
With just a mention.

-     Lighthouse

I'll swim across the salted sea.
Detox the demons within me.
I'll pray on every rose, that hasn't froze,
For love and peace.
Across the mountains, on the beach,
Restless waters carry me,
Through the setting sun,
Near the coast,

En Paradis

WATERLUST (INTRODUCTION

Bm
Into my waters
Freezing and blue
My growing powers
Double in two
G
Chemicals Of change
Alter my mind
F#m Let evolution
Flow with the tides

from F# to Bm
senza il creatività ✦

Bm
Do you do you
Do you wanna
Dive in the sea?
C
your last
Bubble of care
drifts up, send it free

F#m
Don't know where
I'm going
Left all on the beach
Let waterlust take over
Stop Me

dance break

Bbm
I'll swim across
Across the salted sea
detox the demons within me
a
I'll pray on every rose that hasn't
Froze for love and peace

This water lust
Carries me, through
Foreign fantasies
Anchors sink the past
Finally free
Finally free
Finally free
Finally free

*is it cold
by S

*fast cel
flying ki

DANCING CEDARS P

~~SINE PLUCKER 2~~

BWUEY PIPES

ANALOG reic-A-Ta

B G C# D

FUTUR

O

Ø

48

I tie anchors to

Every destructive habit, every regret that never brought me higher truths, that never brought happiness, but an illusion of grandeur to fill voids. Tying ropes around every negative thought that inhibits growth with hidden intentions to distract me from my path. With the weight of the unwanted world on my shoulders, the negative energies that choke me are all thrown overboard, sinking into the darkest trench, never seeing the light of day.

-   Abyss

Wrap melodies around each place,
Around each, every suntanned face.
Pulling words from waters,
Picking limes and riding waves.

With his glow, Apollo,
Shower me with golden rays.
Promise you'll never leave me,
Like a star that never fades.

Chariots through oceans,
Water colored in the frame.
Into arms, you lift me up
In dreams, I levitate.

- Apollo

Swimming off the coast.
Pouring honey on my wounds.
Skin glistens in the light,
In my eternal youth.
Everything's on fire,
Until I meet the moon.
Coloring the sky,
With my deepest blues.
Mountains reaching high,
Energies suffused.
Slowing down the time,
Warm in my solitude.
Impressions, summer wine,
Riviera watered hues.
Bergamot and lime,
Head high, I'm
Falling through.

-     Portofino

Creative currents,
Freeing, flowing,
Towards the blue lagoon.
Not too rigid, waters frigid,
I know to dive in soon.
Calculations, caring too much,
Narrows what could be.
Letting loose, do not confuse,
Intentions, set them free.

-    Free Flow

Swimming through the currents in my veins,
In the wilds of the isles, up the curve of my back.
Diving deeper into myself to find the chest
Of treasures, locked. With the golden key,
My will, to unlock every answer waiting,
And every question, every cloud will clear.
Sun shining on my golden skin,
In paradise.

-    Treasure Island

A mans time to think for himself.
A mans time to forgive his past.
A mans time to flood the wounds,
to stand on his own, to drown all the wreckage.
A mans time to rise from the water,
to ride on the waves that crash and reform.
A mans time to stroke the chords of freedom,
to sink through the surface, to then be reborn.

-    Oceanus

Fountains of tears,
Filled for years,
Of wishes, hope
And worried fears,
Pour out the mouths
Of cherubs, stoned.
Flipping coins
In waters, cold.

- In bocca al lupo

Slipping through the melting sun,
Shooting their words like fired guns.
But I couldn't hear through the
Thunder of the moment,
Just my heart racing faster
Than I could ever run.
With my head high off hope,
Into the Roman streets,
With every angel inching
Closer, glowing in all my

Broken Glory

In dark dusk,
On the balcony,
Whispers in the night,
Every secret, high and low
That echoed through our lives.
Where hearts were ripped with
Bullets, all the sculptures stare and sit.
They never feel the piercing pain of
Pleasures, poisoned tricks.
Champagne pirouettes, the cigarettes
That smoke the highest hill, in Rome,
Laying back in all our stars,
Writing more thrills.
Nothing lasts forever.
Our perceptions always change.
I never have the answer, all I know is

Life Is Strange

I write to remember,
The rise and the fall.
The thorns, all the
Damage, divine
Conscious calls.
I write to capture
Each feeling,
Each tear and
Each breath,
That left from
My lungs so I'll
Never forget.

-       Non Lasciarmi

Lips made of marble, solid heart.
Placed, a part of the museum.

Sculpted to be left, a statue, posed,
Nothing more to all these guests.

In life, although as a masterpiece,
Nothing but still, nothing to feel.

Cold to the touch, unable to cry,
Left in this life, immortalized.

- Do You Feel Real?

Taking trains so far away,
From my mind, to newer states.
Acclimate and then erase,
Heart pounding in the station.
They greet me with a smile, spark,
Off the rails, out of the dark.
New worlds, unseen,
Those violet streams,
Leading through
The night.

-   Ciao

Amethyst on my bone,
Red velvet eyes, stoned.
Holding hands with strangers,
In our watered worlds combined.
Drunk and stumbling near the saints,
In the twisted ways we've paved.
Flirting with danger,
Disappeared in the night.

-      Foreign Friends

FEELING X

no coordinates
for restless hearts

that want too
much but where
to start?

Higher self from the future,
Bears visions marking higher growth.
In his shadow, in Milano,
Breaking my bones, feeding the flames.
Drawing madness from within,
Manifesting into physical.
Words spun from my mind,
Like thread to his design.
Writing over and over
In hopes that maybe,
It'll all be worth my while,
My creations can glow,
Before time erases me.

-    Comme Gianni

If my soul wasn't split in two,
I wouldn't have to look for you.

Too young to know but want it all,
Touching in the sunshine view.
Trace intentions 'round your eyes.
Leading in, I fall right through.
Rushing towards each other,
To taste all what we think we need.
Desires burn, underneath shirts,
Hidden from city streets.
Make a wish, before the darkness
Covers the perfumed park,
Before the final petal falls,
We bloomed to be forgotten.

-    confused admirers (?)

Que lingua
Seu coração fala?
What's the code
To crack
Quel est le ton
De la voix,
That resonates
Con la tua anima?
Que cultura
Qué gesto
Qué camino
Do I have to speak,
Per te da capire
Quanto mi importa

-     Lost in Translation

Flourish when touched, buds open up,
Burn when flames melt us together.
Skins reflect and ambers glow.
Indomitable nature,
Poisoned pleasures.
But the rarest touch,
Could only melt the ice,
Replete desires,
Lover to lover, us

Boys of Paradise

On my best days
When you're around,
I wear dark light,
Let ambers glow.
Through your arms,
Through the park,
Mind fully wrapped
Around your soul.
On blackest days,
The ambers stay.
With just one spray,
I'm not alone.
To remember
Then, each
Moment spent,
Like golden coins
In fountains cold.

-    Dark Light

Pressuring fate, can't bear to wait,
For messages, vibrations, aching days.
Alone, my thoughts like
Daring dragons,
Torching logic, choking the truth.
Overthinking, my rational
Pities the heart that obsesses,
That stresses the empty details,
The minuscule bits of nothing.
I'm anxious, I'm running, let
My lungs give up, defeated in this

Waiting Game

Too much caffeine,
Strung out and running.
Possessed, nerves shot.
Climbing up the closing walls,
Attached for just a message.
Melting in Milano's sun,
Waiting. Waiting. Waiting.
Different scene's
Yet similar feelings,
Longing, obsessing,
Regretting.

-    Old Habits Die Hard

Every bone left broken,
Cathedrals crumble down.
You sent me flying,
'Till you clipped my wings, came,
Crashed into the ground.
All the arrows ripping
Through places, touched,
But bleed so blue.
Translating madness
Into melodies,
To heal the wounds
From you.

-    dov'è il tuo amore?

Stringing stars to light the
Darkest path. Locking
All the doors that open to
Feelings full of hate.
The lowest lows,
Follow the highest highs.
My bleeding heart
Has its cuts, though it
Still beats. I try to feel
As alive as I can,
But the more I pay,
The more my pockets
Drain to empty holes.

-      everything has its price

I always say the wrong thing when I fail to open up. Always do
The wrong thing when I try, it's not enough. I know how to
Change, writing mantras, try to grow up. Still swimming in the
Ice, in my cruel youth, narcotic rush. I think I have the
Answers, the key, until I'm wrong. Always push my best, be
Perceived as if I am strong. Keeping all my demons in lines,
Right by my side. Like gold around my neck, wear mistakes with
All my pride.

-    Cruel Youth

Still
SWIMMING
IN THE ICE,
IN MY
CRUEL
YOUTH
narcotic rush

Spinning all the thread,
Through my skin, I stitch.
Fell from the highest hope,
Pleasures pains are a bitch.

-    Pleasures Pains

80

We all have hopes
we all have dreams
that tie us down to
certain things. Like beautiful
bous and diamond rings
wrapped around our fingers
But scissors come to cut the
cloth. We all have our shares
of loss. Trapped inside our
hearts and heads. Living
other lives instead

X X

Each memory made, worsens the weight,
Of the fall, when everything's erased.
Still I trace, each, every place,
I went to feel that highest state.
But now I'm falling through the space,
Where we went to light our flames.
Though I knew your touch was danger,
You'll always be my favorite stranger.

-    Favorite Stranger

It's hard to see through the storm
When you're blinded by the clouds.
It's hard to be high, when you know
You're coming down.
It's hard to breathe easily,
When there's pollution in the air.
It's hard to be infatuated
When we know you never cared.
It's strange to live a newer
Life then be stuck back at square one.
It's strange the past eats away
At everything I've ever done.
And only memories remind me
Of everything I've ever felt,
While the ghosts of all I've loved,
Fly into the sun and melt.

Or maybe, it's not that serious.
I need to catch my heart,
It's had too much to dream.
Drunk off delusions, beating impatiently,
it traps what it can get, eating expectations,
daggers fall. But everything is easier,
when I don't try to have it all.

Losing to tempting tastes of trouble,
Distract to destroy,
Indulge to enjoy.
Saving for tomorrow,
All the problems that thunder,
When my mind is under the

Influence

Why do you rush to tomorrow?
Why can't you sit in today?
Why can't you be in the present moment?
Why do you wish it away?
Why do you busy yourself for hours?
Why do you send problems to sleep?
Why can't you stop waiting for,
What will simply never be?

I taste bitter like cinnamon,
Cold eyes that could cut.
In days without color,
Left writing in blood,
On walls that surround me,
Circle round the edge,
Of the glass that I smash
When I'm lost in my head.

I taste bitter like cinnamon,
Burn lavender fields,
No laying in gardens,
Too frozen to feel.
Mindfulness holds
The mirror I shatter,
When my thoughts are scattered,
At midnight, battered and torn.

- Cinnamon

Head turned from responsibilities.
Slipping on my delusions out
The doors of passing possibility.
All direction lost with wings
Too broken to keep flying.
Diamond pleasures, powdered blue.
Falling further into a trench.
Leaving stores shining in luxury,
Practicing for the next life.
But there is nothing left.
No money, no home,
Nothing to turn to
And suddenly it hit me,

What the fuck am I doing with my life?

Excitement surpassing exhaustion.
Hope surpassing fears.
On the veins of the tracks
Moving far from here.
Conversations with strangers,
Converged cultures new,
Replace who I had been,
Removed me far from you.

-    Midnight Train

TO TRAINS
TO TAXIS
TO PLANES
TO ~~YOU~~
FORGET

I try to grab as much as I can
With the changing world
Spinning before me.
I try to make some sense,
To have a taste,
To learn something,
To belong somewhere.
But I don't belong anywhere
When I've been uprooted
Too many times.
Losing myself with strangers
And disappearing so often,
It's almost as if, my home
Is in the planes, the trains,
The subways, that take
Me anywhere, but here.

-    Itinerant Identity

Le passé, est oublié
Retour a l'endroit où j'ai commencé
Mon lit vide, mon visage rayonne
Ce qui frappe moi plus
Ce comment que tu
As tiré mes roses from the roots
Mais tout grandit après le tempête
En Ville, En Ville, En Ville,
Avec tout les filles
Avec tout les garçons
Qui ne connaissent pas mon nom.
Gold swinging from my neck.
Letting myself forget, Where I'm from
When the sun burns down.
Now I know, all alone,
Passing dark cafés,
Lights glow, through the streets
En Paris now.
Champagne scenes, sparkling,
Higher than the Eiffel dreams,
Lace my boots,
Je vais en ville now
Diamonds in my mouth,
Rainbows in my eyes,
Dancing with strangers,
Lit, technicolored skies,
Left him, left it behind,
Je ne regrette rien,
Roses fall from heaven,
Kiss the moon
And meet the sun.

-     EN VILLE

94

En
ville

En ville

En ville

En ville

En ville

En ville

The chemicals making their way
Down my body in stranger states
And new cities, with Florence
Spinning on the table, turning all my tears
To cyclones that keep us apart.
Six hours ahead, in stoned streets, old.
I sew each word to repair, release,
Record, the rapid change in me.
Hallowed out my chest,
But still, never forgetting.

-    Ever Evolve

CHEMICALS OF CHANGE

Forget each life with every tear I shed, and the faces in the subway turn the other way instead. Odd, unsure how to feel, as each second hits my face, somehow, I feel so raw when I'm far out of place. Each passing look, each written hook, breaks a part of me, then mends me even stronger with every word I bleed. And I tried to make sense of my new self throughout the streets, maybe the light was too bright before for me to ever see. In those rarest moments, I'm bleeding from my soul. Roses cut my skin, from my body they grow. Sober yet never felt as high as I feel, above meeting angels with wings made of steel.

- Uomo Nuovo

vines of roses,
endless doses,
warm embraces,
hidden places.
hanging mirrors,
reflect visions,
intuition leads decisions.
chaos, silenced.
sleeping violence.
Oceanus waves,
light, sacred state.
all alone,
always, forever,
across the seas on

holiday

My life is like a painting,
Set into the scene,
Still in colored oils,
Inside a drying dream.

Eyes that light one hundred lives,
For centuries, I'll remain.
Portray the bullets in my chest,
The blood around the frame.

- Forever Feeling

Each note, word wrote,
Shreds the grief.
The coils break to detach me
From what I know is worst,
But I still gripped by the neck,
Until it snapped and then
There's nothing for me
to hold on to.

Such a foreign feeling,
With empty hands.
With nothing at all.

-    Detaching

The world is bending
Back to everything I know,
Or at least thought I knew.
But newer eyes, suggest
That it's all old.
With my altered mind,
Chemistry different
And the ghosts that
Still surround me
From everywhere I went,
Everyone I've been.

-    Mindfuck

INTUITION

Truth without explanation
link to higher self
Transcends body, mind and spirit
Chakra 6

Intellect · (trust) · Intuition

Faith

Faster than physical world
patience · trust · concentration
translates into physical realm
match with <u>action</u>
honor past self to honor intuition
· act upon your visions ·

INTUITION LIVES IN THE FUTURE

All knowledge known, yet to be known.
All answers wait, to be unlocked.
Intuition leads to destined worlds,
To higher realms, the higher self.
In the silence, deepest state,
Of consciousness, destiny waits.
Doubts erased, won't hesitate,
To trust, lead to the truth.

- Intuition

The truth is wrapped around
What's been forbidden,
Yet naturally inviting,
To simply take a bite.
The apple tastes so good,
Just because you told me,
Not to eat it.

\-   *The rise.*

moralities imposed from the outside,
had never fit me quite the same,
as others, conforming, unaware,
don't question, raise their voice.
living in the darkness
shifts my soul into the purest light.
though no one goes, fears to expose,
what's hiding in the night.

-     Under Lies

Breaking the patterns.
Breaking my mind.
Breaking the habits,
Of whom I have been.
Acknowledge the faults.
Acknowledge the cracks,
Acknowledge the behaviors,
That led to dead ends.
Washing the ink,
Clean from the paper.
Acknowledge the fractures,
Start over again.

- Mind Break

As you turn inwards,
Realizing everything
We need is inside
Instead of focusing
On external factors,
We begin to cultivate
An entire regenerative
Process in uncovering
Our next evolutionary
Step. We are unable
To grow until we
Learn to drop our
Underlying, limited
Beliefs and recognize
Our perfection as is.
When we focus on this path
We will naturally harvest
Our infinite potential
And continue to grow,
With all our chains,
Finally relinquished.

No more hallucinations of hope.
Plunged from the depths of desire.
It's difficult to rework, rewire
What's been conditioned for so long.
It is a process of constantly
Peeling each layer of myself,
Wiping the dust from the mirror
To see the true, bare reflection
Of whom I was from the beginning.
Untouched and pure.
I don't want what you want for me.
I want what I want for me.
Everything else, will be shed,
Ignored, washed away, no
Longer a face full of flames,
Searing with confusion.

-    Rising

We have all been corrupted in the guise of purification.
We have all been brainwashed from the beginning,
Numbing, aching, straining our innocence, for years.
There is no such thing as right and wrong.
Opinions are not the truth,
But you were not taught to handle the truth.
It takes everything we have been taught thus far,
It takes the greatest strength, the rip of every muscle
To take what we have been given and throw it over a cliff.
Only then you can rise into higher consciousness.
Only then you will know.

Living on the internet,
Where all morals are freed.
Technology evolved,
Killing off reality.
Cyber auras glowing,
Blending false with what is real.
In entirely new worlds,
Where we still love
And lie and steal.

-   Cyber Aura

these eyes.
these glares.
these needles.
these stares.
this scope.
this digital disease of the mind.
these programs.
these judgments,
these attempts,
to impress.
to formulate yourself,
superior than others.
this digital void,
this meaningless exhaustion,
the superficial, artificial reality.
these followers, bred,
left them on read
and close my

digiteyes

Turning off the broadcast,
Had been the hardest thing
For me to do, despite hearing
Nothing but static on the other end.

-    Power Off

When I lose myself,
I look for violet lights.
Always there,
Behind every melody,
Behind every question,
Behind every illusion.
I'll fill each streetlight
With violet, leave every
Place glowing, knowing
That everything is perfect.
Everything is in place.

-    signs

Open your mouth.
Spit the truth out
Like venom, before
It poisons you.
Leave nothing unsaid.
All that's been raging
To ring out for years.
Enough of biting my tongue.
Whatever's said, is done.

– SPEAK UP

Angels dance and love and laugh, light as feathers of wings. Bearing gifts, laid out in clouds with gold and diamond rings. Life is light in fragments of my mind that strive to breathe, when I'm away from hades, on Olympus, choirs sing.

I can choose the path most traveled, no worries at all. Filling cups with wine, another cherub on the wall. But I'm not blind to thorns piercing the flesh of humanity. I know full well the blood that's spilt on earth from wars and greed. I would risk the bliss, the golden gates in lighter scenes, to come back down and flood the pain, bring light to everything.

If my wings are clipped trying to save another soul, let my name be known, undying love preserved in gold.

-    Martyr

One body to another, always sharing with
each other. Feelings caught, then thrown into
the fire, start again. We taste what we all starve for
in one night then disappear. Addicted to conflicting thoughts.
Love?
Lust?
It's all unclear.

-     Lonely Lovers

With violets come venom,
With beauty comes pain.
Addictive afflictions,
But am I to blame.
All this violet venom,
Running through my veins.
Violet venom, love and hate,
Deadly nightshade, ice and flames.
One comes not, without the other,
Falling under, lonely lovers.

-    Violet Venom

Into the violet fire,
Every thought starts to expire.
Extracting all the poison
From my veins, the worry, drained.
Turning inwards, turning axis,
To what I failed to ever access.
Torching every torturer.
Alone, in love with it.

-      Venus in Flames

Freedom hurts.

Everyone chases after anything, or anyone,
to distract them from acknowledging themselves.
To drop out of the human race and face their
essence, their inner chaos. They are weak,
running out of fear that they are really nothing,
but a question of existence.

Those who are brave enough to stop distracting themselves, turn inwards to face the chaos of agony. To turn 180 degrees into the deepest part of yourselves, falling into the trench of your chaos, is painful, uncomfortable. The truth hurts, removing one from all comfort, from all distractions, removing masks, occupations used to cover your identity, to face the very essence of your being. Your purpose. Your true place. Your acceptance of nature and your willingness to allow it to take its course over your life, rather than straining to force a desired reality. By cracking the shell of agony, ecstasy is born, every question will be answered. Everything is bliss. To find yourself, is to find everything.

- Agony + Ecstasy

Never living in the present,
Lost in all that's still unknown.
The present pulls me back,
My pools of patience, overflown.
Sending wishes to the water,
Dreams, they race when fate's asleep.
Seconds pound the futures locket
When uncertainty swallows the key.

-    Anxiety

visions, mirrors,
reflect again,
as I evolve
and understand.
who I am,
who I could be,
each potent possibility.

what I do,
what I think
cannot grow,
without both linked.
action called,
I'll give my all,
to bring to new reality.

- Visions

Tears in silver streams,
Carry everything, down the mountains
Of my mind, in violet water springs.
Every sleeping dream, will awaken,
see the light, mirroring my visions,
proving I was always right.

- In Time

Normal is an illusion.

There is no right or wrong. There is no normal. The word "normal" is
an empty word that people fill with their expectations, their own preferences, their
own insecurities, disguising it as what should be "normal" or "right." Some people
fear those who do not fit their expectations, their lifestyle, their assumed sexuality,
their gender roles. They are afraid. They do not possess the tolerance, the open mind
and hide behind this term. There is no normal, only free will and the right to self-
expression.

The right of freedom.

In the dimension of endless wonder,
With no restrictions, but the freedom
to move out of forms and recreate again
and over, whoever I am, whoever I'll be.
Unbound by the physical, freed from flesh
And drained of blood, no muscles nor bones
To call a home. who am I then, where do I exist?

- Immaterial

Born from the dark,
Unafraid to slay,
Eyes like lightning,
Breathing flames.
Hands in mudras,
Protect love and peace.
Rip every demon,
Piece by piece.
Through black light,
Through every scene,
Remove what poisoned everything.
Lick the blood of fallen fiends,
Through violent storms,
To violet springs.

- Kālarātri

It's as if the future writes itself
And I read unknowingly,
Unaware, unapplied,
Until I suddenly meet
The moment, everything clicks.
It's almost a sort of
Psychic reading,
A violet blueprint,
How intuition, aligns all the stars
Before the night even falls

– violet prints

This barren, stripped ocean floor I've laid in for months, has unlocked infinite potential. The void, where energies collide, fade, rebuild, has burst into glorious manifestation. The beginning blueprints of the next phase take place in the void as revitalized energies break down the present. Action in physical reality starts unleashing new tides at perfect timing, flooding with waters of a new life, finally rehydrated. The process of change is delicate and balanced. There can be no resistance which stagnates this flow of energy.

You either move with the current and accept it, or you are pulled into undertows and drown.

- **THE VOID**

WAVES PULL BACK TO
VIEW THE VOID, ENERGY
CREATED TO BE DESTROYED
WHAT LIT MY EYES WITH
STARS OF JOY, FADE BACK
INTO OBLIVION

I went as far as I could get.

Riding, flying forever. Running away from comfort. Chasing something that sends my anxiety spiraling, leaving me with an insatiable thirst, to drink what I have not yet seen, to be someone I have not yet been. Forever restless. I went as far as I could get. Past the mansions and the seas. Past the churches and the bars, old and new. Living out of suitcases, running to train platforms to take me elsewhere. With each place, moment of grace, alone throughout the veins of each country, writing and erasing myself. Letting every crystal tear drop into each street, to remind that I was here. I went as far as I could get.

But I'm not far enough yet.

time again, to test the waters.
time again, refuse to stay.
time again, detach and fall,
not fall to all illusions of change.
waters rush through city streets,
subways bullet underseas.
muscles ache, move through days
and trust, that I'll survive.

-    Is It Cold In The Water?

In the overwhelming
Sea of energy, on the island
In the concrete jungle with
Strangers, passing faces
Filling what had been lost.
Unsure of what it costs
To start over again.
The hearts of millions
Beating under my breath.
This new energy lights up
Every building, every streetlight,
Writing deep in Central Park.

-    New Energy

You're a luxury I'm trying to afford.
The earth breaking through the boards.
The light in every city sign,
The half that fills the other side.
The one dropping bombs, blowing my ice,
Most addictive, pure and willing vice.
Smoking through each wilting wish,
To live a moment twice.
Meeting up to break me down,
To sugared beaches, golden brown,
Melting in your hands,
Couldn't care about the world.

     -     At First

Take the M,

Moving slow, up the curve of your back.

Take the L,

When you leave and reality smacks.

Words can relieve, relive moments like facts,

Still you shocked me out of my skin.

At 11,

I'm rushing to meet in the dark.

At 3 though,

You dam me, I'm blown with a spark.

In the taxi I'm shattered, tear signals apart.

When you call, I'm ready to go.

- 3AM

I still don't know
What it means to be myself.
When I change so fast,
And feel like someone else.
Whom I never seem to recognize,
Trace everywhere I've been.
Flowers wilt, what does it mean,
To even be human?
The lives I've lived too long,
Eventually must die.
People break from me,
Left alone, under the sky.
What if I forget myself?
My thoughts, all my dreams,
And shift into a stranger who
Likes and works for different things.
The essence there, I hope and trust
Through time I'll still survive,
Through constant deaths,
All the rebirths of these

100 lives

MIRRORS IN BARS
IN DIFFERENT CITIES
REFLECTING A STRANGER
I DON'T SEEM TO RECOGNIZE
HE FOLLOWS ME WHEREVER
I GO, WITH HIS BURNED
BROWN EYES, A FOREIGN
FRIEND, TRAILING BEHIND
TO MEET AGAIN

coromandel screens
and perfumed dreams,
to cover over everything,
to bring you closer into me,
to stop the pounding future.
leading me with dirty wings,
an angel from a foreign scene.
lit, into the midnight streets,
warming up your ego.
felt the fever in my head,
dying in your desert end.
I'll forgive and I'll pretend,
we're fine, only,
just friends.

- coromandel

I had a dream I followed you
into the woods at night, but I couldn't
keep up. Reaching out to find you, I cut
my hand, a beating pain in dread as I
pulled my phone to flash a light, showing
the vines of roses all around me with thorns
sharp and shining red, running with blood.

- subconcious signals   8.11.19

142

In between what I thought and what is clear.
Strung out, on edge, a trembling ego.
But nothing can succeed the nature of truth,
Amid desires and what I've been led into,
What I thought to expect, I was caught.
Leading me on, deep into the dungeons of your damages.
Unaware of your actions, your behavior, your cruel nature.
But who am I to point out the cracks, the fractures?
Broken but though, the only position is to accept what is clear
And to lay in this emptiness, to teach myself
To not force change on others anymore.
To not place expectations on them.
To not hold them up to certain standards and
Project hopeful realities onto the inapplicable.
To have no cravings attached, which pulls suffering
From the tenures of my tendencies.

Have it your way.

Foreign tongues
And foreign faces
Foreign touch and
Foreign places.
Familiar feelings
I suspect, and still
I tried to break my neck.
For loneliness, I tried to kill.
For emptiness, I tried to fill.
Sunken in the summer haze.
Disappeared, I'm

Godless

My heart and head,
Don't think the same
One falls to logic,
The other, pain.
One overthinks,
One feels too much.
But they meet once,
They both get crushed.

-     Tug of War

Eyes rolling over words
That I've heard a hundred times,
I've got things to think about and
I can't have you on my mind.
Breathing steam and rising
From the fog you set me in.
I've got better things to do,
Letting a new era begin.

The snake around my body
Never lets me lose a fight.
You want to ride with me
But do you think you'd last a night.
Eyes rolling over words, that
I've heard a hundred times,
I've got things to think about
And I don't want you in my life.

- Sever

Into the springs,
in the steam, under leaves,
of the palms, of the hands,
that were there in my sleep.

Heated, the dreams, that rolled
like beads, of sweat down my back,
I've removed what I need.

I opened the thought of a
love that could stay.
Entertained as it flew,
far off and away

Into springs, in the steam,
now I need nothing,
but the sun, done is done,
I've escaped.

     -    Solito

Our paths have been paved further from each other.
Unable to enjoy the simplicity, the joy of each laugh,
When there was nothing then to worry about.
Now we're chasing each day before it slips from our hands,
In different cities,
As different people.

-      Forgotten Friends

Brooklyn, boys,
Professions and pleasures,
chase minutes until the day ends.
Night falls, underneath lights,
in bars where vices dare.
Underneath a hundred mirrors,
Influence of a draining glass.
Tensions build between two
bodies, into sleepless nights.

- Business & Pleasure

Through the rigid edges lining the path of this journey, sacrifices must be made in some form or another to further growth. Persisting passions, cravings and restlessness signaled my timing to drop all I've known. Friends to be left, family to let go, familiar places to farewell. There is no other option for those who honor themselves, truly, and do not refuse their potential.

Comfort is removed, into nights alone in swallowing cities, baring teeth begging to bite. The path is difficult, lonely, cruel, but I cannot silence my intuition. I cannot silence myself.

I don't dream. I work.

It doesn't matter, about your art.
If there's no feelings left.
It doesn't matter, your aching heart,
Beating in your chest.
In violet springs, all will bloom,
With the power to believe.
In autumn nights, winds whip through,
I fall again like leaves.

-     Relapse

A party boy,
With eyes that cut,
Falling pills,
Disguised as luck.
Know better, but no remedy
For broken boys,
With tired dreams.

A wild boy,
No longer fragile,
Lovely thrills,
The brightest smile.
In the darkest hour,
I confess, I'm still,
I'm going numb.

- The Fall

On the balcony of the building, watching people run blind like ants. Losing themselves in their routines. Work. Home. Rest. Work. Not truly knowing themselves, moving further from their essence. They don't know what to want, looking towards others for fulfillment, for any form of entertainment. Refusing to acknowledge reality. My patience never stays too long as I slip through their words and back into my thoughts. I don't bother surrounding myself with people who distract me from myself, who take but never give, merely just robots in their surroundings. The candles have burned down and darkness fills the room. Finally, alone, I can breathe

HIKIKAMORI 引き籠り

I don't need silence,
My mind is my madness.
My laugh is my sadness.
My smile's my pain.

The seconds are slipping,
Into the voices,
White pills and choices,
To always run wild.

Telling then turning,
Into the burnings,
Always relearning,
To put back the pieces.

Black is my day sky.
Clouded, I stay high,
Lost in dark currents, at

4AM

You're addicted to your suffering
You're proud to let it show,
You drag the sun to hell
dance in flames to have it known.

You're addicted to your misery
and you don't want a hand,
To save you from your drowning,
Far away from summers sands.

No longer a victim,
I've grown out of the way,
That poisons hope,
I've flipped a switch to
Breathe a brighter day.

You thrive in the shadows,
But there, I can't remain,
Higher in my state of bliss,
Wish you could feel the same.

-       Higher Observations

Is this the beginning of
The end of the earth,
Burning our worth,
Through forests, love's hurt.
Is this the beginning,
Of the promised end,
Power in wrong hands,
Blood spilling again.

In essence, comprised,
The sum of same hearts,
Still beating apart,
Broken and dark.
Hope is the only thing
Left still to keep,
Dangerously steep,
With me, until

The End of The Earth

There's nothing left,
I try my best to feel alive.
Hurts to confess,
The strength of hate is idolized.
Another cloud over the sun,
Bloody streets, violence undone.
Needing peace, to feel relief,
With every fighting try.

Everywhere I go, relentless ghosts
Remind me who I've been.
When I trace the city's streets,
I was falling into him.
But everything goes,
No matter how I hold tight.
Words get caught inside my throat,
Melt in the heat, melt in your eyes.

Voices rage through cities,
Lost you through the country's lines.
Nothing will be the same,
I'm just trying

To Feel Alive

New York is hot
And tension fuming in the air.
The growing split between
The just and the unfair.
The facts of life,
Collective consciousness is one,
But torn when bodies fall in streets
By war and fired guns.

The tears that run and rage,
Building in bodies race.
Never rest, never content
'Till justice bears the weight.
Every night, a hope for change
Leads me into sleep.
In better realms,
Where everything is perfect

In My Dreams

Retreats into the self
Underneath these violet waters.
Going back towards the center after
Running rampant for so long.
Each breath can lead the way back
From wars so dark and violent, anxiety
Drips in winters, running red.
I shut everything out. I listen. I breathe. I meditate,
I pull myself back through fogs of feelings and my worries of the world.
I could cause every fracture, but I can mend with every solution.
I cannot forget my breath, no matter how many I give.
I cannot forget purpose, no matter how many lives I live.

One day I'm high by turquoise waters,
Some days in clouds of grey.
I try to act the best in hopes
That all I love can stay.
Impermanence embraced,
Still carried away the best,
Of what I thought was right for me,
But now I've passed the test.
Identified, though I admit,
Dark tendencies run deep,
Trials train self-worth
To finally end

The War in Me

One thousand eyes on me before,
One thousand hands pulling for more.
One thousand thoughts to tear logic
To pieces, closing doors.

One thousand voices silenced,
One thousand days to find the floor,
Restructured, standing stronger,
Coming down in black Dior.

– Black Dior

The deeper I descend the more it is realized that happiness is nothing but a fleeting illusion. A momentary high that proceeds with some eventual fall.
Permanent happiness cannot even be possible, an unrealistic goal.

The deeper I descend the more it is realized, to stop telling myself that I "should" be happy. I should not be anything but a mindful state, greeting and letting go of each passing feeling, understanding their messages and waving them off.

There is no higher choice but to accept whatever state we are in and to not feel uncomfortable when we feel nothing at all. We merely reach an equilibrium, a peace with accepting these states, then returning to an emptiness.

A contentment in nothing.

Nothing Is Everything.
Everything Is Nothing.

No feelings left to keep.
No taste of cruel defeat.
No thorns surrounding me,
When time leaves me to see.

No more wounds to show.
No pain left as I grow.
Surrendered, vulnerable,
I've learned,

The Art of Letting Go

Pressing to switch perception,
As I flip through every day, like
The pages of a book, I begin
To tear away.
Ripping towards the end,
Now I'm left with shredded pieces,
Like a puzzle never cared for,
Enjoyed, nor completed.
Unable to stop, what's
Said, still never done. Forever
A sociopathic sucker on the run.
But there's nothing any city
Could ever give to me,
Than what I find within
To bring me full relief.

-    Repair + Release

The more I depend,
The more I bend,
To wills, none of mine.
Draining distractions
And breaking connections,
Wasting energy at night.

When I pull away,
Some friends come back,
Full grown as they all prove,
The gold in the wreckage
Of all that I left.
The bonds I'll never lose.

- The Deep End

Not change of place
But change of mind,
Needed to make worth of time.
To make some sense
To bring forth peace,
To still the rumbling, starving sea.

- The Liberating Wave

Fireworks pouring from my eyes,
High against the skyscrapers
As I strip myself again of
All that held me down.
No intentions, no more
Chasing empty chalices.
Appreciating what I have,
What I have accomplished,
Rather than being unsatisfied.
Living with only the
Desire to enjoy each moment.
To let each smile and touch
Ignite more violet flames,
Glowing forever,
Illuminating the darkest hour.

    -    Fulfillment

NO BONE
OF DOUBT
NO MUSCLE
OF FEAR

Floating through the fumes,
In the roads, throughout the city.
Against the colors of the buildings,
On the rooftops of hotels.
Diving off the shores,
Rum running down my mouth,
With the suns blinding rays,
Dripping, pouring down.
Everything slow motion,
Pass the glittered, colored cars.
Kids running through the streets
As time breaks inside the lounge.
Inhale the cities secrets,
Skin warm and cinnamon.
A wanderer in all the glorious
Worlds I'm living in.

- La Habana Vieja

I am just a wanderer,
Finding my way, in and out of every
Culture, surrendering comfort, losing myself
Through the days and maybe something
Will lead to another and opportunity
Will blossom. With no compass
With no more goals, but the strength
To surrender to nature,
Letting myself be swept away
In all the beauty, all the
Wonders of the world.

-    Wanderer

Dove's fly from my chest,
Above the cracking ground,
God's on fire in the light,
In my burning rebirth.
New cells,
New hands,
New eyes,

Throwing roses into
The fountains of my soul,
For every test, passed,
For every moment of doubt,
For every broken bone,
Mended, in perfect timing.

In perfect alignment, with the universe.

My life comprises of fractured waves and spinning compasses; of numbing thoughts that stretch into the blank expanse of the horizon, fizzling into oblivion. My life comprises of memories sealed in glass bottles and thrown overboard, floating away from remembrance.

My life comprises of lost laughs, flickering faces, intoxicated states and bonds that break the bounds of time. Retracing each day, each place on maps that lead from one country to the next, one moment to the other, the what was to what is. I follow the dots that guide this voyage, without knowing the destination, without knowing what X marks the spot.

My life comprises of sailing beyond the unknown, floating forever or crashing and capsizing. There is no trajectory, no direction. With fleeting memories of all that I have experienced. Held, treasured, let go.

-    Feeling X

Life tore me up like paper,
Up the walls, out of my mind.
Stillness in the early hours,
Before the calm declines.
Worries, fears, fill the room,
from thoughts left on rewind.
Playing, but I navigate through
storms to white sunshine.
The cycle is over, left
amid the middle summer's heat.
Quieting my mind,
as waves again recede.
Burn words into the sky,
into futures I can't see.
Letting go of love, of cities,
Now not meant for me.

-      End Cycle

I've been here before. I've lived in every star on stage, in other writers on a page. I see parts, pieces of what I feel in them, who've had to risk it all, trusting their intuition, refusing failure. We block out every feeling of doubt, sacrificing security for the moments our red flames of effort turn violet, as people are touched, enlightened by our words, our music, our art. Those moments we taste the nectar of our bloomed flowers, is the richest, closest feeling of godliness we could ever feel.

- purpose

Maybe no one will ever hear your songs, know your thoughts, view your perspective. Maybe no one will read your story, but that doesn't mean it does not hold value. When everyone is sleeping in the dark, your flames will still burn, fiercely, authentically, infinitely.

Just because I write everything,
Does not mean I know everything.
Sometimes, I just place running
Thoughts on a page, learning from
Each source, implementing, practicing,
Experiencing each concept, each perspective.
I have the dignity, the respect to say,
Just because I'm knowledgeable,
Does not mean, I *know.*
Because I don't know.
I am always in a process of questioning,
Learning, accepting what serves me
And rejecting what does not.
Once I finally understand, every question
Will disappear. So, I just read, I listen, I watch.
I'm nothing, but an

Observer

Intuition led me out of comfort.
Intuition led me into new worlds.
Intuition led me into my words.
Intuition led me to every song.
Intuition led me into new arms.
Intuition led me into my truth.

You see me in violets,
You see me in light,
You see me in diamonds,
24k white.

You see me as ashes,
But always the truth.
You see me as simply,
An extension of you.

- Soul Inseparable

When the last arrow
Has been shot
Through clouds,
The last piece
Of gold rains down.
Virtue rewarded,
Vices shredded,
At peace near
The end after
The road had
Been paved.
Nothing stays,
Lay my body in

Champs-Élysées

This is my best,
This is my worst.
Take all I am,
All that I'm worth.
What I needed,
Now forgotten,
What had died,
Now reborn

-     La fin

I live my life,

Following intuition, ignoring principles, fueled by passion, trusting my instinct. Finding freedom in working, manifesting each thought into a physical masterpiece. Living authentically with no doubts of my identity. Ignoring formalities, rejecting opinions of others and what is said to be normal. Building an entirely new world from the ashes of the past. Transforming my rebellion into my creations and letting them glow with the flames of a thousand suns. Desiring what has not yet been thought of. Always testing myself. Always working. Always daring and continuing to push myself every day.

I will go on,
Evolving, flying,
Failing, flying,
Succeeding, knowing
Not knowing,
Writing, creating,
Until I have fulfilled
My highest potential.
Then everything will be
Completely wiped away.
Everything will stop,

At the final exhale.

To whomever had taken the time to read this book,
thank you for allowing me to share my thoughts,
my pain, my madness, my lessons learned. I hope
in some way, you have taken something
with which you can apply to your own life.
Trust yourself.
Trust your intuition.

Works by the writer

Books
Water (2016)
Intuition (2020)

Music
Break Apart – Single (2017)
Violet Nights – EP (2018)
Ares (Revenge) – Single (2019)
En Ville – Single (2020)

www.violetvenom.com

IG: @AKADomm @violetvenomx